Young George Washington ran down the hill from the house to the dock so fast he almost plunged into the blue waters of the Potomac before he could stop.

The great sailing ship coming up the river was preparing to drop anchor.

Ocean-going vessels often passed his half-brother Lawrence's plantation on the way to the busy little port of Alexandria. It was eight miles farther upstream. Only once or twice a year did one stop at the plantation. It must be something important.

"Could it be bringing a letter from Admiral Vernon saying that you may name your plantation after him?" asked George when Lawrence joined him.

Lawrence looked puzzled. "I only wrote to him a few months ago," he said. "That is hardly enough time for an answer. Maybe some of the friends I met when I served under the admiral in the West Indies are coming."

When the captain came ashore he handed Lawrence a letter and a big square box.

"Admiral Vernon asked me to deliver these to you on my way to Alexandria," he said.

Lawrence broke the seal and read the letter quickly.

"You were right, George!" he said. "The name of my plantation can now be *Mount Vernon.*"

Lawrence asked one of the servants standing on the shore to carry the box to the house and asked George to see that it was opened carefully. Then he turned to chat with the captain.

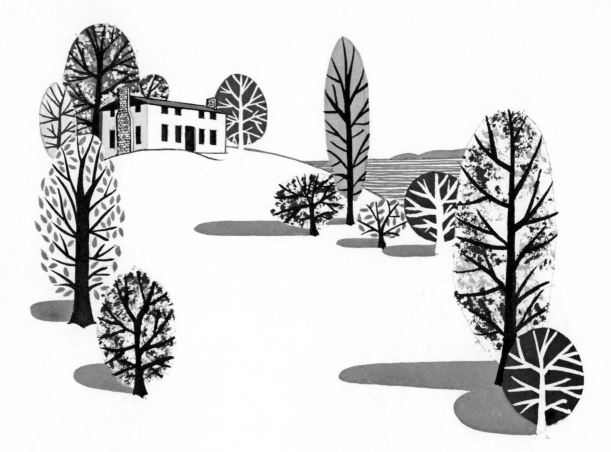

As George climbed the hill he wondered what Admiral Vernon would think of the plantation named in his honor, if he could see it.

The white, wooden house Lawrence recently had built for his bride was small. It looked like an oblong box. It was only a story-and-a-half high. There were four rooms and a center hall downstairs and four rooms and a hall above.

As George waited beside the house for the servant with the box, he looked out over twelve miles of shining river. The green shores of Maryland, across the Potomac, stood out clearly in the sun. He felt certain that the view would make up for any shortcomings the admiral might see in the house. George thought it was the prettiest spot in all the Virginia colony.

He wished his father had rebuilt the house that had burned down on that spot. Instead the family had moved to Ferry Farm. Just before he died, his father gave the twenty-five-hundred-acre plantation to Lawrence.

The servant, huffing and puffing, set the box before George. Together they uncrated a fine wrought-iron lantern.

Later, George helped Lawrence hang it in the hall-way. Over two hundred years have passed and the lantern is still there.

When George was fifteen he moved to Mount Vernon to live with Lawrence and his wife.

For the next five years life on the plantation was gay and carefree. There were many parties and social gatherings among the neighbors and George made many lasting friends.

He studied surveying and practiced it by surveying all of Mount Vernon's rolling green acres.

In 1752 there was sorrow in the little house. Lawrence died, and his wife moved back to her former home.

A sad and lonesome George Washington became the master of Mount Vernon when he was twenty years old.

Before he had time to get used to his new responsibility he was called into the king's colonial army. He rode off to fight the French and Indians on the frontier.

For seven long years the little house waited for its master's return. The paint grew gray and the foundations began to crumble. When Washington came home for visits he found the place lonely, and rode off to stay with friends.

One day a rider brought a letter to the servants that changed the whole future of the plantation. The master was bringing a bride home to Mount Vernon!

She was the wealthy young widow, Martha Dandridge Custis. He asked that the house be put in good condition for her, and her two small children.

Friends from neighboring plantations came to help. Carpenters and masons came. Foundations were rebuilt and a third floor was added. Gleaming white paint made the house look like new.

Workers sang as they did the spring planting.

The cook found recipes that had been George's favorites.

The young couple and the children arrived one bright spring day in 1759. The rich earth smelled moist and fresh, and dogwoods splashed the woods with pink and white.

As their great coach rounded a bend, they could see the house high on its hill. It looked like a gleaming jewel on a bright green mat.

It was much smaller than the mansion Martha had left. But she smiled happily as she went from room to room. When she saw the lovely view of the shining river she gasped with pleasure.

"We will build a porch clear across the front of the house someday," George promised her.

One of the first things the young couple had to do was order furniture from England. Lawrence's wife had taken hers with her, and George had not had time to replace it.

They did not have catalogs as we do today. They had to write and tell just what they wanted and hope that the agent would make a good choice.

On their first order they asked for such things as "one neat and easy sofa for a passage," and "four fashionable china branches for candles."

Both Martha and George liked things "simple and neat, but fashionable and of the best quality."

After Washington became famous, an admirer sent him a fancy marble mantel. There is a story that pirates stole it on its way from England. When they saw it was addressed to Mount Vernon, they risked their necks to deliver it.

Washington wrote, "It is almost too fancy for my taste." But it was fashionable and of the best quality, so one day he put it in the new banquet hall when it was added to the house. It is still there today.

For a second time the little house became a happy home. Its rooms rang with the laughter of the children and the bustle of everyday living.

George set about making his plantation one of the best in the colonies. He bought more land and divided it into five farms. Each had its own servants' quarters, stables and cattle.

He built fishing stations along the river, and a mill to grind his grain. He experimented with soils and crop rotation.

Soon the merchants in England looked forward to products from Mount Vernon, for they knew they would be of the best quality.

Martha took pride in seeing that everything that had to do with the house ran smoothly. Every morning, wearing a frilly white cap, she visited the neat white cabins behind the main house, where the household chores were done.

The kitchen cabin was closest to the house. Its fireplace was large enough to hold a bed. Spicy dried herbs hung from the ceiling within easy reach of the cook. Huge warming pans and iron kettles hung on the walls.

Martha's children often went with her on her morning rounds. They soon learned that the crock in the kitchen corner was always full of cookies. They found the servants in the nearby dairy house, churning tubs of butter, were happy to hand out fresh milk to go with the cookies.

They held their mother's hands when she went in the spinning and weaving cabins, but they kept away from the wash house. They knew that the hot, bubbly

soapsuds and the steam that hissed through the door might burn them.

The smoke house was the only one that was silent. Great hams and sides of beef hung motionless as they aged to just the right degree of tastiness.

Gradually more neat white cabins grew behind the big house. Blacksmiths, cobblers, brickmakers and other craftsmen moved in. The plantation was like a little village, able to take care of all its needs.

19

Martha often watched for the great sailing vessels from England to bring her pretty crystal or the latest fashions. George looked for special seeds and rare cuttings from the farmers abroad.

Life at Mount Vernon settled into a pleasant pattern that the Washingtons followed all their lives, even after they became famous.

George rose with the sun and often lighted the fires in the fireplaces himself. He worked on plans and accounts until nine o'clock. Then he ate his favorite breakfast of hoecakes and honey and rode off on his big horse to inspect his farms.

He returned at the same time each day to change for dinner. It was served promptly at three in the afternoon!

They never ate alone. Relatives, friends, and strangers gathered around the gleaming mahogany table.

The distances between inns were long and the roads were poor, so travelers were always welcome.

The army of little Negro boys running between the kitchen and main house with steaming platters of food never knew how many they would be serving.

Unless there were special guests, George went to bed at nine o'clock. That was the hour supper was served! Martha stayed up with the others while they enjoyed the juicy hams and rich cakes.

George and Martha loved company. Mount Vernon soon became the favorite place for the neighbors to gather for a gay round of fox hunting, cards, and dancing. A neighbor was anyone on either side of the Potomac within a day's travel.

Mount Vernon had the finest horses and hounds in the countryside. In the early mornings the woods echoed with the sound of the hounds and the horns as men in bright waistcoats chased the fox.

In the evenings, candles glowed softly as ladies in long silk gowns danced the stately minuet with men in satin knee britches.

The house always seemed at its best when it was full of company. The walls almost seemed to stretch to make them comfortable. But it was during the evenings of dancing that George realized his house was too small.

One day he brought carefully drawn plans to Martha showing how he wanted to enlarge it.

"There will be a banquet hall on this end, two stories high," he explained. "To balance it, we will build a library with a master bedroom above it on the other end.

"The porch I promised you, will have eight columns reaching to the roof. There will be room for at least thirty chairs so our friends can admire the view. Will that be enough?"

Martha looked up at her tall husband and smiled happily.

In 1773, workmen began building the new wings on the house. Work went slowly, for materials were hard to get from England.

King George had imposed so many unjust taxes and laws on the colonists they talked of rebelling. In 1775, they asked Washington to lead the colonial troops to fight against the king.

For a second time, the master of Mount Vernon rode away to war. He would not return for several years.

This time the house did not stand forlorn and forgotten. It played a special part in the Revolutionary War.

The house was in constant danger of being destroyed by the enemy. But Washington left careful instructions that the building program must continue. He made arrangements for a rider to bring him reports each week wherever he might be.

Even during the winters when Martha joined her husband at his headquarters, Mount Vernon was kept open for travelers. Glowing fires and good food welcomed them as always.

Word passed quickly among the soldiers that General Washington was making expensive additions to his plantation on the Potomac. They saw him writing long letters of instructions to his overseer each week.

When the fight for independence looked hopeless, the soldiers watched to see if he stopped the work on his house. Defeat would mean he would lose his home to the enemy. Instead of stopping the building, he wrote urging the workmen to hurry the job.

General Washington's faith in the future inspired his weary fighting men. Mount Vernon became a symbol of hope to them. They felt that as long as their leader continued to build, there was a chance they could win the war.

On Christmas eve, 1783, candles glowed from every window of Mount Vernon. Bonfires blazed in the servants' quarters. The war had been won! The master was coming home after eight long years.

George was glad to settle down to the pleasant ways of the plantation again. Two of Martha's grandchildren came to live with them, and it seemed like old times except on a grander scale.

George finished the wings and the porch he had begun before he went away. He built greenhouses for his exotic plants and a formal garden marked with spicy boxwood hedges. He made his daily trips around his farms.

He found time to stop at the little garden house the children used for a school, to hear them recite. He was never too busy to listen to a new piece that little Nellie had learned on the harpsichord he gave her.

Both Washington and his house still had important roles to play in American history. He was considered the first citizen of the new country and Mount Vernon was looked upon as his official residence.

On its pleasant porch, delegates planned the first steps for uniting the colonies in their independence from England.

In the new library, hundreds of letters were written to persuade important men to vote for the Constitution.

Under its roof, Washington received official notice he had been elected President of the United States.

When he returned in 1797, after serving two terms as president, he was world famous. Politicians, generals, historians, and foreign dignitaries flocked to Mount Vernon.

The house had grown into a mansion, but it had not lost its air of gracious simplicity that had made the neighbors feel welcome years before.

One miserable, rainy day Washington caught cold, while visiting his mill. Two days later, on December 14, 1799 he died. He was buried in the family vault near the house.

After Martha died in 1802, the plantation was divided among twenty-three relatives. George's nephew, Bushrod Washington, inherited the house.

For sixty years the mansion was handed down in the Washington family. Because there was not enough land with it to raise crops, there was not enough money for repairs.

Fifty years after George died, the porch roof had to be propped up with a ship's mast. The paint had peeled and the cabins behind the house had collapsed. The greenhouses had been flattened by fire, and the gardens were choked with weeds.

During all the years, a constant stream of visitors came to see the house where the first citizen lived, and to bow their heads reverently before his tomb. Ships passing on the Potomac tolled their bells in his honor.

Other mansions made of stronger materials disappeared from the landscape. But Mount Vernon seemed to be waiting — waiting as though it knew it still had a part to play in American history.

In 1860, the long wait ended. A group of patriotic ladies formed the Mount Vernon Ladies Association of the Union. They bought the neglected mansion to restore it.

29

With loving care they pored over Washington's papers to find out everything they could about the house. They wanted to make it as much as possible like it had been when he lived there.

They repaired and painted the main house, rebuilt the neat white cabins, and replanted the pretty gardens.

They ordered new flagstones for the porch from the same quarry in England that Washington had used. They were delighted to be given some bricks, that were made when he was alive, to rebuild the greenhouses.

Gradually the ladies have collected some of the articles and furniture that belonged to Martha and George. They are proud of the big four-poster bed that the Washingtons bought while he was president. It is the one in which he died.

The harpsichord he gave his granddaughter, and the flute he never learned to play, are in the music room. His spyglass and his globe are in the library. Almost every room has something in it that belonged to the famous couple.

Through lots of study and work the mansion has been restored.

Now many, many people take the pleasant boat ride down the Potomac from the city of Washington, or drive by car, to visit it.

The charming simplicity of colonial days lingers on, and the visitors feel as though Martha and George are waiting to greet them around the next corner.

Mount Vernon is America's most famous and beloved shrine. It seems only proper that the crews of all naval vessels salute and lower the flag to half mast, while taps are played in passing the home and tomb of America's first citizen.